Tortilla Soup Cookbook

A Collection of Delicious and Creative Recipes Inspired by the Classic Tortilla Soup

While every precaution has been taken in the preparation of this book, the publisher assumes no responsibility for errors or omissions, or for damages resulting from the use of the information contained herein.

TORTILLA SOUP COOKBOOK

First edition. January 25, 2024.

ISBN: 979-8224504282

Written by john ahmad.

Table of Contents

John Ahmad

Chapter 1: Introduction to Tortilla Soup

Welcome to the flavorful world of tortilla soup! In this chapter, we'll delve into the history, cultural significance, and share valuable tips for creating the perfect tortilla soup in your own kitchen.

1.1 History and Origins of Tortilla Soup

Tortilla soup has a rich history that can be traced back to the culinary traditions of Mexico. It is believed to have originated in the central and southern regions of the country, where it has been enjoyed for generations. We'll explore the roots of this beloved dish and discover how it has evolved over time.

1.2 Importance of Tortilla Soup in Various Cuisines

While tortilla soup has its roots in Mexican cuisine, it has also gained popularity worldwide and is now enjoyed in various culinary traditions. We'll explore the influence of tortilla soup in other cuisines, such as Tex-Mex, Southwestern, and even fusion interpretations. You'll discover how this humble soup has become a versatile and beloved dish across different cultures.

1.3 Tips for Making the Perfect Tortilla Soup

Now that we understand the historical and cultural context, it's time to dive into the practical aspects of making a delicious tortilla soup. In this section, we'll share valuable tips and techniques to ensure your soup turns out flavorful and satisfying every time. From selecting the right ingredients to mastering the cooking process, these tips will elevate your tortilla soup game.

Choosing the Base: We'll discuss the various options for the base of your tortilla soup, such as tomato-based, broth-based, or creamy bases. We'll highlight the flavor profiles and provide guidance on selecting the best base for your desired outcome.

Essential Ingredients: We'll explore the key ingredients that give tortilla soup its distinct taste, including tortillas, tomatoes, onions, garlic, and spices. You'll learn how to balance these ingredients and make substitutions when needed.

The Art of Broth: Broth plays a vital role in the flavor foundation of tortilla soup. We'll guide you on making homemade broth and offer recommendations for store-bought alternatives. We'll also provide tips on enhancing the depth of flavor using herbs, spices, and aromatics.

Perfecting the Texture: Achieving the ideal texture is essential for a satisfying bowl of tortilla soup. Whether you prefer a smooth and creamy consistency or a slightly chunky texture, we'll share techniques to achieve your desired result.

Garnishes and Toppings: Tortilla soup is incomplete without its signature garnishes and toppings. We'll explore traditional and creative options, such as crispy tortilla strips, avocado, lime wedges, cilantro, cheese, sour cream, and more. You'll learn how to balance flavors and textures to create a harmonious and visually appealing presentation.

Serving Suggestions: We'll provide insights on serving tortilla soup as a standalone meal or as part of a larger spread. You'll discover complementary side dishes, bread options, and beverage pairings that elevate the overall dining experience.

By the end of this chapter, you'll have a solid understanding of the history and significance of tortilla soup, as well as the essential tips and techniques to create a delightful bowl of this beloved dish. So, let's get ready to embark on a flavorful journey through the world of tortilla soup!

Chapter 2: Classic Tortilla Soup Recipes

In this chapter, we'll explore classic tortilla soup recipes that celebrate the authentic flavors of Mexico. From traditional Mexican-style variations to options using different types of broths, we'll provide you with a range of delicious recipes to satisfy your tortilla soup cravings. Additionally, we'll share tips for garnishing and serving these delightful bowls of soup.

2.1 Traditional Mexican-Style Tortilla Soup
Recipe: Traditional Mexican-Style Tortilla Soup
Ingredients:

- 2 tablespoons vegetable oil
- 1 medium onion, finely chopped
- 3 cloves garlic, minced
- 2 tomatoes, diced
- 1 jalapeño pepper, seeded and minced
- 6 cups chicken or vegetable broth
- 2 cups shredded cooked chicken
- 1 teaspoon ground cumin
- 1 teaspoon chili powder
- Salt and pepper to taste
- 4 corn tortillas, cut into thin strips
- Vegetable oil for frying tortilla strips
- Optional garnishes: avocado slices, lime wedges, chopped cilantro, sour cream, shredded cheese

Instructions:

1. In a large pot, heat the vegetable oil over medium heat. Add the onion and garlic, and sauté until the onion becomes translucent.
2. Add the diced tomatoes and jalapeño pepper to the pot. Cook

for a few minutes until the tomatoes start to soften.

3. Pour in the chicken or vegetable broth and bring the mixture to a boil. Reduce the heat and let it simmer for about 15 minutes to allow the flavors to meld together.

4. Add the shredded chicken, cumin, and chili powder to the pot. Season with salt and pepper to taste. Simmer for an additional 10 minutes.

5. While the soup is simmering, prepare the tortilla strips. Heat vegetable oil in a separate pan and fry the tortilla strips until they become crispy and golden brown. Remove them from the oil and place them on a paper towel-lined plate to drain excess oil.

6. Ladle the tortilla soup into bowls. Top each bowl with a handful of crispy tortilla strips and any optional garnishes you desire, such as avocado slices, lime wedges, chopped cilantro, sour cream, or shredded cheese.

7. Serve the soup hot and enjoy!

2.2 Variations using Chicken, Beef, or Vegetable Broth
Recipe: Chicken Tortilla Soup
Ingredients:

- 2 tablespoons vegetable oil
- 1 medium onion, finely chopped
- 3 cloves garlic, minced
- 2 tomatoes, diced
- 1 jalapeño pepper, seeded and minced
- 6 cups chicken broth
- 2 cups shredded cooked chicken
- 1 teaspoon ground cumin
- 1 teaspoon chili powder
- Salt and pepper to taste
- 4 corn tortillas, cut into thin strips
- Vegetable oil for frying tortilla strips
- Optional garnishes: avocado slices, lime wedges, chopped cilantro, sour cream, shredded cheese

Instructions:

1. Follow steps 1-4 of the Traditional Mexican-Style Tortilla Soup recipe.
2. Proceed with the remaining steps to complete the soup.

Recipe: Beef Tortilla Soup
Ingredients:

- 2 tablespoons vegetable oil
- 1 medium onion, finely chopped
- 3 cloves garlic, minced
- 2 tomatoes, diced

- 1 jalapeño pepper, seeded and minced
- 6 cups beef broth
- 2 cups cooked shredded beef
- 1 teaspoon ground cumin
- 1 teaspoon chili powder
- Salt and pepper to taste
- 4 corn tortillas, cut into thin strips
- Vegetable oil for frying tortilla strips
- Optional garnishes: avocado slices, lime wedges, chopped cilantro, sour cream, shredded cheese

Instructions:

1. Follow steps 1-4 of the Traditional Mexican-Style Tortilla Soup recipe.
2. Proceed with the remaining steps to complete the soup, replacing chicken broth with beef broth and shredded chicken with shredded beef.

Recipe: Vegetable Tortilla Soup
Ingredients:

- 2 tablespoons vegetable oil
- 1 medium onion, finely chopped
- 3 cloves garlic, minced
- 2 tomatoes, diced
- 1 jalapeño pepper, seeded and minced
- 6 cups vegetable broth
- 2 cups assorted chopped vegetables (such as bell peppers, zucchini, corn, and carrots)
- 1 teaspoon ground cumin
- 1 teaspoon chili powder
- Salt and pepper to taste
- 4 corn tortillas, cut into thin strips
- Vegetable oil for frying tortilla strips
- Optional garnishes: avocado slices, lime wedges, chopped cilantro, sour cream, shredded cheese

Instructions:

1. Follow steps 1-4 of the Traditional Mexican-Style Tortilla Soup recipe.
2. Proceed with the remaining steps to complete the soup, replacing chicken broth with vegetable broth and shredded chicken with assorted chopped vegetables.

2.3 Tips for Garnishing and Serving

When garnishing your tortilla soup, feel free to get creative! Experiment with different combinations of avocado slices, lime wedges, chopped cilantro, sour cream, and shredded cheese. These garnishes add a burst of freshness and additional flavors to your soup.

For a healthier twist, you can opt for baked tortilla strips instead of fried ones. Simply brush the tortilla strips with a little oil, season with salt and chili powder, and bake in a preheated oven at 350°F (175°C) until crispy.

To serve tortilla soup as a complete meal, you can add additional ingredients like black beans, corn kernels, or diced potatoes. These additions make the soup more filling and satisfying.

Tortilla soup pairs well with warm corn tortillas or crusty bread on the side. These can be served plain or with a spread of butter or flavored olive oil for an extra touch.

Remember to adjust the seasoning according to your taste preferences. Feel free to add more spices, herbs, or a dash of hot sauce to intensify the flavors.

By following these classic tortilla soup recipes and incorporating the garnishing and serving tips, you'll be able to enjoy a delicious bowl of authentic Mexican-inspired goodness. So, get ready to savor the rich flavors and comforting textures of these delightful tortilla soups!

Chapter 3: Creamy Tortilla Soup Creations

In this chapter, we'll explore a collection of creamy tortilla soup recipes that offer a luscious and velvety texture. These variations incorporate ingredients like cream, cheese, or coconut milk to create a luxurious and indulgent experience. Get ready to savor the richness and depth of flavors in these delightful bowls of creamy tortilla soup.

3.1 Creamy Tortilla Soup with Roasted Corn
Recipe: Creamy Tortilla Soup with Roasted Corn
Ingredients:

- 2 tablespoons vegetable oil
- 1 medium onion, finely chopped
- 3 cloves garlic, minced
- 2 tomatoes, diced
- 1 jalapeño pepper, seeded and minced
- 2 cups roasted corn kernels
- 6 cups chicken or vegetable broth
- 1 cup heavy cream
- 1 teaspoon ground cumin
- 1 teaspoon chili powder
- Salt and pepper to taste
- 4 corn tortillas, cut into thin strips
- Vegetable oil for frying tortilla strips
- Optional garnishes: sliced avocado, lime wedges, chopped cilantro, crumbled queso fresco

Instructions:

1. In a large pot, heat the vegetable oil over medium heat. Add the onion and garlic, and sauté until the onion becomes

translucent.

2. Add the diced tomatoes and jalapeño pepper to the pot. Cook for a few minutes until the tomatoes start to soften.
3. Stir in the roasted corn kernels and continue to cook for another 2 minutes.
4. Pour in the chicken or vegetable broth and bring the mixture to a boil. Reduce the heat and let it simmer for about 10 minutes.
5. Using an immersion blender or regular blender, puree the soup until smooth and creamy.
6. Return the soup to the pot and stir in the heavy cream, ground cumin, and chili powder. Season with salt and pepper to taste. Simmer for an additional 5 minutes.
7. While the soup is simmering, prepare the tortilla strips. Heat vegetable oil in a separate pan and fry the tortilla strips until they become crispy and golden brown. Remove them from the oil and place them on a paper towel-lined plate to drain excess oil.
8. Ladle the creamy tortilla soup into bowls. Top each bowl with a handful of crispy tortilla strips and any optional garnishes you desire, such as sliced avocado, lime wedges, chopped cilantro, or crumbled queso fresco.
9. Serve the soup hot and enjoy the rich and creamy goodness!

3.2 Cheesy Tortilla Soup with Chiles
Recipe: Cheesy Tortilla Soup with Chiles
Ingredients:

- 2 tablespoons vegetable oil
- 1 medium onion, finely chopped
- 3 cloves garlic, minced
- 2 tomatoes, diced
- 2 poblano chiles, roasted, peeled, seeded, and chopped
- 6 cups chicken or vegetable broth
- 1 cup shredded Monterey Jack or cheddar cheese
- 1 cup milk
- 1 teaspoon ground cumin
- 1 teaspoon chili powder
- Salt and pepper to taste
- 4 corn tortillas, cut into thin strips
- Vegetable oil for frying tortilla strips
- Optional garnishes: chopped fresh chiles, sour cream, chopped green onions

Instructions:

1. In a large pot, heat the vegetable oil over medium heat. Add the onion and garlic, and sauté until the onion becomes translucent.
2. Add the diced tomatoes and roasted poblano chiles to the pot. Cook for a few minutes until the tomatoes start to soften.
3. Pour in the chicken or vegetable broth and bring the mixture to a boil. Reduce the heat and let it simmer for about 10 minutes.
4. Using an immersion blender or regular blender, puree the soup until smooth.
5. Return the soup to the pot and stir in the shredded cheese, milk, ground cumin, and chili powder. Season with salt and pepper to

taste. Simmer for an additional 5 minutes, stirring occasionally until the cheese is melted and incorporated.

6. While the soup is simmering, prepare the tortilla strips. Heat vegetable oil in a separate pan and fry the tortilla strips until they become crispy and golden brown. Remove them from the oil and place them on a paper towel-lined plate to drain excess oil.

7. Ladle the cheesy tortilla soup into bowls. Top each bowl with a handful of crispy tortilla strips and any optional garnishes you desire, such as chopped fresh chiles, a dollop of sour cream, or chopped green onions.

8. Serve the soup hot and enjoy the creamy and cheesy goodness!

3.3 Coconut Milk Tortilla Soup with Shrimp
Recipe: Coconut Milk Tortilla Soup with Shrimp
Ingredients:

- 2 tablespoons vegetable oil
- 1 medium onion, finely chopped
- 3 cloves garlic, minced
- 2 tomatoes, diced
- 1 jalapeño pepper, seeded and minced
- 1 can (14 oz) coconut milk
- 6 cups chicken or vegetable broth
- 1 pound shrimp, peeled and deveined
- 1 teaspoon ground cumin
- 1 teaspoon chili powder
- Salt and pepper to taste
- 4 corn tortillas, cut into thin strips
- Vegetable oil for frying tortilla strips
- Optional garnishes: sliced avocado, lime wedges, chopped cilantro, red pepper flakes

Instructions:

1. In a large pot, heat the vegetable oil over medium heat. Add the onion and garlic, and sauté until the onion becomes translucent.
2. Add the diced tomatoes and jalapeño pepper to the pot. Cook for a few minutes until the tomatoes start to soften.
3. Stir in the coconut milk and chicken or vegetable broth. Bring the mixture to a boil, then reduce the heat and let it simmer for about 10 minutes.
4. Add the shrimp to the pot and cook for 3-5 minutes, until the shrimp are cooked through and pink.
5. Stir in the ground cumin and chili powder. Season with salt and

pepper to taste. Simmer for an additional 5 minutes.

6. While the soup is simmering, prepare the tortilla strips. Heat vegetable oil in a separate pan and fry the tortilla strips until they become crispy and golden brown. Remove them from the oil and place them on a paper towel-lined plate to drain excess oil.

7. Ladle the coconut milk tortilla soup into bowls. Top each bowl with a handful of crispy tortilla strips and any optional garnishes you desire, such as sliced avocado, lime wedges, chopped cilantro, or red pepper flakes.

8. Serve the soup hot and enjoy the creamy and tropical flavors!

By exploring these creamy tortilla soup recipes, you'll indulge in the richness and velvety texture they offer. Whether it's the roasted corn, cheesy chiles, or the delightful addition of coconut milk and shrimp, these variations will take your taste buds on a delicious journey. Enjoy the comforting and luxurious experience of creamy tortilla soup in each spoonful.

Chapter 4: Spicy and Bold Tortilla Soup Variations

In this chapter, we'll dive into a collection of spicy and bold tortilla soup variations that are perfect for spice lovers and those who crave intense flavors. These recipes feature chili peppers, spices, and unique seasonings that add a fiery kick and depth to your soup. Get ready to ignite your taste buds with these flavor-packed bowls of tortilla soup!

4.1 Spicy Chipotle Tortilla Soup
Recipe: Spicy Chipotle Tortilla Soup
Ingredients:

- 2 tablespoons vegetable oil
- 1 medium onion, finely chopped
- 3 cloves garlic, minced
- 2 tomatoes, diced
- 1 chipotle pepper in adobo sauce, minced
- 6 cups chicken or vegetable broth
- 1 cup canned black beans, rinsed and drained
- 1 cup corn kernels (fresh or frozen)
- 1 teaspoon ground cumin
- 1 teaspoon chili powder
- Salt and pepper to taste
- 4 corn tortillas, cut into thin strips
- Vegetable oil for frying tortilla strips
- Optional garnishes: sliced avocado, lime wedges, chopped cilantro, diced red onion, crumbled queso fresco

Instructions:

1. In a large pot, heat the vegetable oil over medium heat. Add the onion and garlic, and sauté until the onion becomes

translucent.

2. Add the diced tomatoes and chipotle pepper to the pot. Cook for a few minutes until the tomatoes start to soften.

3. Pour in the chicken or vegetable broth and bring the mixture to a boil. Reduce the heat and let it simmer for about 10 minutes.

4. Stir in the black beans, corn kernels, ground cumin, and chili powder. Season with salt and pepper to taste. Simmer for an additional 5 minutes.

5. While the soup is simmering, prepare the tortilla strips. Heat vegetable oil in a separate pan and fry the tortilla strips until they become crispy and golden brown. Remove them from the oil and place them on a paper towel-lined plate to drain excess oil.

6. Ladle the spicy chipotle tortilla soup into bowls. Top each bowl with a handful of crispy tortilla strips and any optional garnishes you desire, such as sliced avocado, lime wedges, chopped cilantro, diced red onion, or crumbled queso fresco.

7. Serve the soup hot and enjoy the fiery and bold flavors!

4.2 Smoky Tortilla Soup with Ancho Chiles
Recipe: Smoky Tortilla Soup with Ancho Chiles
Ingredients:

- 2 tablespoons vegetable oil
- 1 medium onion, finely chopped
- 3 cloves garlic, minced
- 2 tomatoes, diced
- 2 dried ancho chiles, seeded and soaked in hot water for 15 minutes, then pureed
- 6 cups chicken or vegetable broth
- 2 cups shredded cooked chicken or beef
- 1 teaspoon ground cumin
- 1 teaspoon smoked paprika
- Salt and pepper to taste
- 4 corn tortillas, cut into thin strips
- Vegetable oil for frying tortilla strips
- Optional garnishes: sour cream, sliced radishes, chopped fresh cilantro, crumbled queso fresco

Instructions:

1. In a large pot, heat the vegetable oil over medium heat. Add the onion and garlic, and sauté until the onion becomes translucent.
2. Add the diced tomatoes and pureed ancho chiles to the pot. Cook for a few minutes until the tomatoes start to soften.
3. Pour in the chicken or vegetable broth and bring the mixture to a boil. Reduce the heat and let it simmer for about 10 minutes.
4. Stir in the shredded cooked chicken or beef, ground cumin, and smoked paprika. Season with salt and pepper to taste. Simmer for an additional 5 minutes.
5. While the soup is simmering, prepare the tortilla strips. Heat

vegetable oil in a separate pan and fry the tortilla strips until they become crispy and golden brown. Remove them from the oil and place them on a paper towel-lined plate to drain excess oil.

6. Ladle the smoky tortilla soup into bowls. Top each bowl with a handful of crispy tortilla strips and any optional garnishes you desire, such as sour cream, sliced radishes, chopped fresh cilantro, or crumbled queso fresco.

7. Serve the soup hot and enjoy the smoky and bold flavors!

4.3 Tangy Green Chile Tortilla Soup
Recipe: Tangy Green Chile Tortilla Soup
Ingredients:

- 2 tablespoons vegetable oil
- 1 medium onion, finely chopped
- 3 cloves garlic, minced
- 2 tomatoes, diced
- 2 cans (4 oz each) diced green chiles
- 6 cups chicken or vegetable broth
- 1 cup cooked shredded chicken or pork
- Juice of 1 lime
- 1 teaspoon ground cumin
- 1 teaspoon dried oregano
- Salt and pepper to taste
- 4 corn tortillas, cut into thin strips
- Vegetable oil for frying tortilla strips
- Optional garnishes: sliced avocado, lime wedges, chopped cilantro, diced red onion, crumbled queso fresco

Instructions:

1. In a large pot, heat the vegetable oil over medium heat. Add the onion and garlic, and sauté until the onion becomes translucent.
2. Add the diced tomatoes and diced green chiles to the pot. Cook for a few minutes until the tomatoes start to soften.
3. Pour in the chicken or vegetable broth and bring the mixture to a boil. Reduce the heat and let it simmer for about 10 minutes.
4. Stir in the shredded chicken or pork, lime juice, ground cumin, and dried oregano. Season with salt and pepper to taste. Simmer for an additional 5 minutes.
5. While the soup is simmering, prepare the tortilla strips. Heat

vegetable oil in a separate pan and fry the tortilla strips until they become crispy and golden brown. Remove them from the oil and place them on a paper towel-lined plate to drain excess oil.

6. Ladle the tangy green chile tortilla soup into bowls. Top each bowl with a handful of crispy tortilla strips and any optional garnishes you desire, such as sliced avocado, lime wedges, chopped cilantro, diced red onion, or crumbled queso fresco.

7. Serve the soup hot and enjoy the tangy and bold flavors!

With these spicy and bold tortilla soup variations, you can satisfy your cravings for intense flavors and spice. Whether you choose the smoky chipotle, the tangy green chile, or the fiery ancho chiles, these soups will ignite your taste buds and leave you wanting more. Enjoy the adventurous and flavorful journey with every spoonful of these delicious tortilla soups!

Chapter 5: Healthy and Light Tortilla Soup Options

In this chapter, we'll explore nutritious twists on tortilla soup that prioritize healthy ingredients and cater to specific dietary preferences. Whether you're looking for low-fat, gluten-free, or vegetarian options, these recipes will allow you to enjoy a lighter version of tortilla soup without compromising on flavor. Get ready to savor the goodness of wholesome ingredients in every spoonful!

5.1 Light and Fresh Tomato Tortilla Soup
Recipe: Light and Fresh Tomato Tortilla Soup
Ingredients:

- 2 tablespoons olive oil
- 1 medium onion, finely chopped
- 3 cloves garlic, minced
- 4 large tomatoes, diced
- 4 cups vegetable broth
- 1 cup corn kernels (fresh or frozen)
- 1 red bell pepper, diced
- 1 teaspoon ground cumin
- 1 teaspoon dried oregano
- Salt and pepper to taste
- 4 corn tortillas, cut into thin strips
- Vegetable oil for frying tortilla strips
- Optional garnishes: chopped fresh cilantro, sliced jalapeños, Greek yogurt or sour cream

Instructions:

1. In a large pot, heat the olive oil over medium heat. Add the onion and garlic, and sauté until the onion becomes

translucent.

2. Add the diced tomatoes to the pot. Cook for a few minutes until the tomatoes start to soften.

3. Pour in the vegetable broth and bring the mixture to a boil. Reduce the heat and let it simmer for about 10 minutes.

4. Stir in the corn kernels, red bell pepper, ground cumin, and dried oregano. Season with salt and pepper to taste. Simmer for an additional 5 minutes.

5. While the soup is simmering, prepare the tortilla strips. Heat vegetable oil in a separate pan and fry the tortilla strips until they become crispy and golden brown. Remove them from the oil and place them on a paper towel-lined plate to drain excess oil.

6. Ladle the light and fresh tomato tortilla soup into bowls. Top each bowl with a handful of crispy tortilla strips and any optional garnishes you desire, such as chopped fresh cilantro, sliced jalapeños, or a dollop of Greek yogurt or sour cream.

7. Serve the soup hot and enjoy the light and refreshing flavors!

5.2 Gluten-Free Chicken Tortilla Soup
Recipe: Gluten-Free Chicken Tortilla Soup
Ingredients:

- 2 tablespoons vegetable oil
- 1 medium onion, finely chopped
- 3 cloves garlic, minced
- 2 tomatoes, diced
- 6 cups chicken broth
- 2 cups cooked shredded chicken
- 1 cup corn kernels (fresh or frozen)
- 1 teaspoon ground cumin
- 1 teaspoon chili powder
- Salt and pepper to taste
- 4 corn tortillas, cut into thin strips
- Vegetable oil for frying tortilla strips
- Optional garnishes: sliced avocado, lime wedges, chopped fresh cilantro, diced red onion

Instructions:

1. In a large pot, heat the vegetable oil over medium heat. Add the onion and garlic, and sauté until the onion becomes translucent.
2. Add the diced tomatoes to the pot. Cook for a few minutes until the tomatoes start to soften.
3. Pour in the chicken broth and bring the mixture to a boil. Reduce the heat and let it simmer for about 10 minutes.
4. Stir in the shredded chicken, corn kernels, ground cumin, and chili powder. Season with salt and pepper to taste. Simmer for an additional 5 minutes.
5. While the soup is simmering, prepare the tortilla strips. Heat vegetable oil in a separate pan and fry the tortilla strips until

they become crispy and golden brown. Remove them from the oil and place them on a paper towel-lined plate to drain excess oil.

6. Ladle the gluten-free chicken tortilla soup into bowls. Top each bowl with a handful of crispy tortilla strips and any optional garnishes you desire, such as sliced avocado, lime wedges, chopped fresh cilantro, or diced red onion.

7. Serve the soup hot and enjoy the gluten-free and flavorful experience!

5.3 Veggie-Packed Tortilla Soup
Recipe: Veggie-Packed Tortilla Soup
Ingredients:

- 2 tablespoons olive oil
- 1 medium onion, finely chopped
- 3 cloves garlic, minced
- 2 zucchinis, diced
- 1 red bell pepper, diced
- 1 can (14 oz) diced tomatoes
- 6 cups vegetable broth
- 1 cup corn kernels (fresh or frozen)
- 1 can (14 oz) black beans, rinsed and drained
- 1 teaspoon ground cumin
- 1 teaspoon smoked paprika
- Salt and pepper to taste
- 4 corn tortillas, cut into thin strips
- Vegetable oil for frying tortilla strips
- Optional garnishes: sliced avocado, lime wedges, chopped fresh cilantro, diced red onion

Instructions:

1. In a large pot, heat the olive oil over medium heat. Add the onion and garlic, and sauté until the onion becomes translucent.
2. Add the diced zucchinis and red bell pepper to the pot. Cook for a few minutes until the vegetables start to soften.
3. Add the diced tomatoes and vegetable broth to the pot. Bring the mixture to a boil, then reduce the heat and let it simmer for about 10 minutes.
4. Stir in the corn kernels, black beans, ground cumin, and smoked paprika. Season with salt and pepper to taste. Simmer for an

additional 5 minutes.

5. While the soup is simmering, prepare the tortilla strips. Heat vegetable oil in a separate pan and fry the tortilla strips until they become crispy and golden brown. Remove them from the oil and place them on a paper towel-lined plate to drain excess oil.

6. Ladle the veggie-packed tortilla soup into bowls. Top each bowl with a handful of crispy tortilla strips and any optional garnishes you desire, such as sliced avocado, lime wedges, chopped fresh cilantro, or diced red onion.

7. Serve the soup hot and enjoy the healthy and delicious medley of flavors!

With these healthy and light tortilla soup options, you can relish the goodness of nutritious ingredients while indulging in the flavors you love. Whether you're looking for a light and fresh tomato soup, a gluten-free chicken option, or a veggie-packed delight, these recipes will satisfy your cravings and keep you feeling nourished. Enjoy the wholesome and satisfying experience of these lighter tortilla soups!

Chapter 6: Seafood Delights in Tortilla Soup

In this chapter, we'll dive into a collection of seafood-inspired tortilla soup recipes that bring a delightful oceanic twist to this classic dish. From succulent shrimp to flaky fish and delectable crab, these recipes showcase the versatility of seafood in creating a flavorful and satisfying tortilla soup. Get ready to embark on a culinary journey through the bounties of the sea!

6.1 Spicy Shrimp Tortilla Soup
Recipe: Spicy Shrimp Tortilla Soup
Ingredients:

- 2 tablespoons olive oil
- 1 medium onion, finely chopped
- 3 cloves garlic, minced
- 2 tomatoes, diced
- 6 cups shrimp or seafood broth
- 1 pound shrimp, peeled and deveined
- 1 cup corn kernels (fresh or frozen)
- 1 red bell pepper, diced
- 1 jalapeño pepper, seeded and minced
- 1 teaspoon ground cumin
- 1 teaspoon chili powder
- Salt and pepper to taste
- 4 corn tortillas, cut into thin strips
- Vegetable oil for frying tortilla strips
- Optional garnishes: sliced avocado, lime wedges, chopped fresh cilantro

Instructions:

1. In a large pot, heat the olive oil over medium heat. Add the onion and garlic, and sauté until the onion becomes translucent.
2. Add the diced tomatoes to the pot. Cook for a few minutes until the tomatoes start to soften.
3. Pour in the shrimp or seafood broth and bring the mixture to a boil. Reduce the heat and let it simmer for about 10 minutes.
4. Stir in the shrimp, corn kernels, red bell pepper, jalapeño pepper, ground cumin, and chili powder. Season with salt and pepper to taste. Simmer for an additional 5 minutes or until the shrimp are cooked through.
5. While the soup is simmering, prepare the tortilla strips. Heat vegetable oil in a separate pan and fry the tortilla strips until they become crispy and golden brown. Remove them from the oil and place them on a paper towel-lined plate to drain excess oil.
6. Ladle the spicy shrimp tortilla soup into bowls. Top each bowl with a handful of crispy tortilla strips and any optional garnishes you desire, such as sliced avocado, lime wedges, or chopped fresh cilantro.
7. Serve the soup hot and enjoy the tantalizing flavors of the sea!

6.2 Creamy Fish Tortilla Soup
Recipe: Creamy Fish Tortilla Soup
Ingredients:

- 2 tablespoons butter
- 1 medium onion, finely chopped
- 3 cloves garlic, minced
- 2 tomatoes, diced
- 6 cups fish or seafood broth
- 1 pound white fish fillets, such as cod or tilapia, cut into bite-sized pieces
- 1 cup corn kernels (fresh or frozen)
- 1 cup heavy cream
- 1 teaspoon dried thyme
- Salt and pepper to taste
- 4 corn tortillas, cut into thin strips
- Vegetable oil for frying tortilla strips
- Optional garnishes: chopped fresh parsley, lime wedges, diced red onion

Instructions:

1. In a large pot, melt the butter over medium heat. Add the onion and garlic, and sauté until the onion becomes translucent.
2. Add the diced tomatoes to the pot. Cook for a few minutes until the tomatoes start to soften.
3. Pour in the fish or seafood broth and bring the mixture to a boil. Reduce the heat and let it simmer for about 10 minutes.
4. Stir in the fish fillets, corn kernels, heavy cream, dried thyme, salt, and pepper. Simmer for an additional 5 minutes or until the fish is cooked through and flakes easily with a fork.
5. While the soup is simmering, prepare the tortilla strips. Heat vegetable oil in a separate pan and fry the tortilla strips until

they become crispy and golden brown. Remove them from the oil and place them on a paper towel-lined plate to drain excess oil.

6. Ladle the creamy fish tortilla soup into bowls. Top each bowl with a handful of crispy tortilla strips and any optional garnishes you desire, such as chopped fresh parsley, lime wedges, or diced red onion.

7. Serve the soup hot and savor the creamy and delicate flavors of the sea!

With these seafood delights in tortilla soup, you can indulge in the fresh and delightful flavors of shrimp, fish, crab, and other seafood delicacies. Whether you prefer the spicy kick of shrimp or the creamy richness of fish, these recipes will transport you to the coastal waters and leave your taste buds longing for more. Dive into the oceanic depths of flavor with these tantalizing seafood tortilla soups!

Chapter 7: International Flavors in Tortilla Soup

In this chapter, we embark on a culinary adventure, exploring global cuisines with unique interpretations of tortilla soup. We'll delve into the flavors of Asia, the Mediterranean, and fusion-inspired recipes that infuse this beloved dish with exciting international twists. Get ready to tantalize your taste buds with a world of flavors in every spoonful!

7.1 Thai Coconut Curry Tortilla Soup

Recipe: Thai Coconut Curry Tortilla Soup

Ingredients:

- 2 tablespoons vegetable oil
- 1 medium onion, finely chopped
- 3 cloves garlic, minced
- 2 tablespoons Thai red curry paste
- 1 can (14 oz) coconut milk
- 4 cups chicken or vegetable broth
- 1 cup diced chicken breast or tofu
- 1 cup sliced mushrooms
- 1 red bell pepper, thinly sliced
- 1 cup snap peas, trimmed
- 1 tablespoon fish sauce (or soy sauce for a vegetarian option)
- Juice of 1 lime
- Salt and pepper to taste
- 4 corn tortillas, cut into thin strips
- Vegetable oil for frying tortilla strips
- Optional garnishes: chopped fresh cilantro, sliced red chili peppers, lime wedges

Instructions:

1. In a large pot, heat the vegetable oil over medium heat. Add the onion and garlic, and sauté until the onion becomes translucent.
2. Add the Thai red curry paste to the pot and stir for a minute to release its aromas.
3. Pour in the coconut milk and chicken or vegetable broth. Stir well to combine.
4. Add the diced chicken breast or tofu, mushrooms, red bell pepper, and snap peas to the pot. Simmer for about 10 minutes or until the chicken is cooked through or the tofu is heated.
5. Stir in the fish sauce (or soy sauce), lime juice, salt, and pepper. Adjust the seasonings according to your taste preferences.
6. While the soup is simmering, prepare the tortilla strips. Heat vegetable oil in a separate pan and fry the tortilla strips until they become crispy and golden brown. Remove them from the oil and place them on a paper towel-lined plate to drain excess oil.
7. Ladle the Thai coconut curry tortilla soup into bowls. Top each bowl with a handful of crispy tortilla strips and any optional garnishes you desire, such as chopped fresh cilantro, sliced red chili peppers, or lime wedges.
8. Serve the soup hot and relish the vibrant flavors of Thai cuisine fused with the comfort of tortilla soup.

7.2 Mediterranean-Inspired Tortilla Soup
Recipe: Mediterranean-Inspired Tortilla Soup
Ingredients:

- 2 tablespoons olive oil
- 1 medium onion, finely chopped
- 3 cloves garlic, minced
- 2 tomatoes, diced
- 4 cups vegetable broth
- 1 cup cooked chickpeas
- 1 cup sliced black olives
- 1 cup diced roasted red peppers
- 1 teaspoon dried oregano
- 1 teaspoon ground cumin
- Salt and pepper to taste
- 4 corn tortillas, cut into thin strips
- Olive oil for brushing tortilla strips
- Optional garnishes: crumbled feta cheese, chopped fresh parsley, lemon wedges

Instructions:

1. In a large pot, heat the olive oil over medium heat. Add the onion and garlic, and sauté until the onion becomes translucent.
2. Add the diced tomatoes to the pot. Cook for a few minutes until the tomatoes start to soften.
3. Pour in the vegetable broth and bring the mixture to a boil. Reduce the heat and let it simmer for about 10 minutes.
4. Stir in the cooked chickpeas, black olives, roasted red peppers, dried oregano, ground cumin, salt, and pepper. Simmer for an additional 5 minutes.
5. While the soup is simmering, preheat the oven to 350°F

(175°C). Brush the corn tortilla strips with olive oil and place them on a baking sheet. Bake for 8-10 minutes or until the tortilla strips are crispy.

6. Ladle the Mediterranean-inspired tortilla soup into bowls. Top each bowl with a handful of crispy tortilla strips and any optional garnishes you desire, such as crumbled feta cheese, chopped fresh parsley, or lemon wedges.

7. Serve the soup hot and savor the delightful Mediterranean flavors fused with the comfort of tortilla soup.

7.3 Fusion Fiesta Tortilla Soup

Recipe: Fusion Fiesta Tortilla Soup

Ingredients:

- 2 tablespoons vegetable oil
- 1 medium onion, finely chopped
- 3 cloves garlic, minced
- 2 tomatoes, diced
- 4 cups chicken or vegetable broth
- 1 cup cooked shredded chicken or grilled shrimp
- 1 cup corn kernels (fresh or frozen)
- 1 cup diced pineapple
- 1 tablespoon soy sauce
- 1 teaspoon ground cumin
- 1 teaspoon chili powder
- Salt and pepper to taste
- 4 corn tortillas, cut into thin strips
- Vegetable oil for frying tortilla strips
- Optional garnishes: sliced avocado, chopped fresh cilantro, lime wedges

Instructions:

1. In a large pot, heat the vegetable oil over medium heat. Add the onion and garlic, and sauté until the onion becomes translucent.
2. Add the diced tomatoes to the pot. Cook for a few minutes until the tomatoes start to soften.
3. Pour in the chicken or vegetable broth and bring the mixture to a boil. Reduce the heat and let it simmer for about 10 minutes.
4. Stir in the cooked shredded chicken or grilled shrimp, corn kernels, diced pineapple, soy sauce, ground cumin, chili powder, salt, and pepper. Simmer for an additional 5 minutes.

5. While the soup is simmering, prepare the tortilla strips. Heat vegetable oil in a separate pan and fry the tortilla strips until they become crispy and golden brown. Remove them from the oil and place them on a paper towel-lined plate to drain excess oil.

6. Ladle the fusion fiesta tortilla soup into bowls. Top each bowl with a handful of crispy tortilla strips and any optional garnishes you desire, such as sliced avocado, chopped fresh cilantro, or lime wedges.

7. Serve the soup hot and enjoy the explosion of flavors from this fusion-inspired tortilla soup.

With these international flavors in tortilla soup, you can take your taste buds on a global journey. From the aromatic spices of Thai cuisine to the fresh and vibrant Mediterranean ingredients, and the exciting fusion fiesta, these recipes offer a diverse range of flavors that will bring a whole new dimension to your tortilla soup experience. Embrace the cultural fusions and let your taste buds travel the world!

Chapter 8: Slow Cooker and Instant Pot Tortilla Soups

In this chapter, we'll explore convenient recipes for busy individuals using slow cookers or Instant Pots. These set-it-and-forget-it methods allow you to effortlessly create flavorful and satisfying tortilla soups while saving time and effort in the kitchen. Whether you prefer the slow and steady cooking process of a slow cooker or the quick and efficient results of an Instant Pot, these recipes will make your tortilla soup preparation a breeze.

8.1 Slow Cooker Chicken Tortilla Soup
Recipe: Slow Cooker Chicken Tortilla Soup
Ingredients:

- 1-pound boneless, skinless chicken breasts
- 1 can (14 oz) diced tomatoes, undrained
- 1 can (10 oz) enchilada sauce
- 1 onion, chopped
- 1 can (4 oz) chopped green chilies
- 2 cloves garlic, minced
- 4 cups chicken broth
- 1 teaspoon ground cumin
- 1 teaspoon chili powder
- 1 teaspoon salt
- 1/4 teaspoon black pepper
- 1 cup frozen corn kernels
- 1 can (15 oz) black beans, drained and rinsed
- 4 corn tortillas, cut into thin strips
- Optional garnishes: sliced avocado, shredded cheese, chopped fresh cilantro, lime wedges

Instructions:

1. Place the chicken breasts in the slow cooker.

2. Add the diced tomatoes, enchilada sauce, chopped onion, green chilies, minced garlic, chicken broth, ground cumin, chili powder, salt, and black pepper to the slow cooker. Stir to combine.

3. Cover the slow cooker and cook on low for 6-8 hours or on high for 3-4 hours, until the chicken is tender and cooked through.

4. Remove the chicken breasts from the slow cooker and shred them using two forks. Return the shredded chicken to the slow cooker.

5. Stir in the frozen corn kernels and black beans. Cover the slow cooker and cook for an additional 30 minutes to allow the flavors to meld together.

6. While the soup is cooking, prepare the tortilla strips. Preheat your oven to 375°F (190°C). Place the tortilla strips on a baking sheet and bake for 8-10 minutes, or until they are crispy and golden brown.

7. Ladle the slow cooker chicken tortilla soup into bowls. Top each bowl with a handful of crispy tortilla strips and any optional garnishes you desire, such as sliced avocado, shredded cheese, chopped fresh cilantro, or lime wedges.

8. Serve the soup hot and savor the comforting flavors of a slow-cooked tortilla soup.

8.2 Instant Pot Beef Tortilla Soup
Recipe: Instant Pot Beef Tortilla Soup
Ingredients:

- 1 pound beef stew meat, cubed
- 1 tablespoon vegetable oil
- 1 onion, chopped
- 1 red bell pepper, chopped
- 2 cloves garlic, minced
- 1 can (14 oz) diced tomatoes, undrained
- 4 cups beef broth
- 1 cup corn kernels (fresh or frozen)
- 1 can (15 oz) black beans, drained and rinsed
- 1 teaspoon ground cumin
- 1 teaspoon chili powder
- 1 teaspoon salt
- 1/4 teaspoon black pepper
- 4 corn tortillas, cut into thin strips
- Optional garnishes: sour cream, diced avocado, chopped fresh cilantro, lime wedges

Instructions:

1. Select the sauté function on your Instant Pot and heat the vegetable oil. Add the beef stew meat and brown it on all sides. Remove the beef from the Instant Pot and set it aside.
2. Add the chopped onion, red bell pepper, and minced garlic to the Instant Pot. Sauté for a few minutes until the vegetables soften.
3. Add the diced tomatoes, beef broth, corn kernels, black beans, ground cumin, chili powder, salt, and black pepper to the Instant Pot. Stir well to combine.
4. Return the browned beef stew meat to the Instant Pot.

5. Close the lid of the Instant Pot and set the valve to the sealing position. Select the pressure cook/manual function and set the timer for 25 minutes on high pressure.

6. Once the cooking time is complete, allow for a natural pressure release for 10 minutes before carefully releasing the remaining pressure.

7. While the soup is cooking, prepare the tortilla strips. Preheat your oven to 375°F (190°C). Place the tortilla strips on a baking sheet and bake for 8-10 minutes, or until they are crispy and golden brown.

8. Carefully remove the lid of the Instant Pot and give the soup a stir. Taste and adjust the seasonings if needed.

9. Ladle the Instant Pot beef tortilla soup into bowls. Top each bowl with a handful of crispy tortilla strips and any optional garnishes you desire, such as sour cream, diced avocado, chopped fresh cilantro, or lime wedges.

10. Serve the soup hot and enjoy the robust flavors of this quick and easy Instant Pot tortilla soup.

With these slow cooker and Instant Pot tortilla soup recipes, you can enjoy the convenience of hands-off cooking while still savoring the delicious flavors of this beloved dish. Whether you prefer the tender and juicy chicken in the slow cooker version or the hearty and savory beef in the Instant Pot version, these recipes are sure to become staples in your kitchen. Embrace the ease of preparation and let your kitchen appliances do the work while you enjoy a steaming bowl of flavorful tortilla soup.

Chapter 9: Vegan and Plant-Based Tortilla Soup

In this chapter, we'll explore plant-powered tortilla soup recipes that are free from animal products. We'll discover creative ways to achieve a rich and satisfying flavor profile without compromising on taste. These vegan and plant-based tortilla soup recipes will not only nourish your body but also delight your taste buds with their vibrant and wholesome ingredients.

9.1 Smoky Black Bean Tortilla Soup
Recipe: Smoky Black Bean Tortilla Soup
Ingredients:

- 2 tablespoons olive oil
- 1 onion, chopped
- 3 cloves garlic, minced
- 1 red bell pepper, chopped
- 1 jalapeño pepper, seeded and finely chopped
- 1 teaspoon ground cumin
- 1 teaspoon smoked paprika
- 1/2 teaspoon chipotle chili powder (adjust to taste)
- 2 cans (15 oz each) black beans, drained and rinsed
- 1 can (14 oz) diced tomatoes, undrained
- 4 cups vegetable broth
- Juice of 1 lime
- Salt and pepper to taste
- 4 corn tortillas, cut into thin strips
- Optional garnishes: diced avocado, chopped fresh cilantro, lime wedges

Instructions:

1. Heat the olive oil in a large pot over medium heat. Add the chopped onion, minced garlic, red bell pepper, and jalapeño pepper. Sauté until the vegetables are tender.
2. Stir in the ground cumin, smoked paprika, and chipotle chili powder. Cook for another minute to toast the spices and release their flavors.
3. Add the black beans, diced tomatoes, and vegetable broth to the pot. Bring the mixture to a boil, then reduce the heat and let it simmer for about 15 minutes.
4. Using an immersion blender or a countertop blender, blend the soup until smooth and creamy. Alternatively, you can leave some of the beans and vegetables intact for a chunkier texture.
5. Stir in the lime juice, and season with salt and pepper to taste. Adjust the seasonings according to your preference.
6. While the soup is simmering, prepare the tortilla strips. Preheat your oven to 375°F (190°C). Place the tortilla strips on a baking sheet and bake for 8-10 minutes, or until they are crispy and golden brown.
7. Ladle the smoky black bean tortilla soup into bowls. Top each bowl with a handful of crispy tortilla strips and any optional garnishes you desire, such as diced avocado, chopped fresh cilantro, or lime wedges.
8. Serve the soup hot and relish the smoky flavors and creamy texture of this vegan black bean tortilla soup.

9.2 Roasted Vegetable Tortilla Soup
Recipe: Roasted Vegetable Tortilla Soup
Ingredients:

- 2 tablespoons olive oil
- 1 onion, chopped
- 3 cloves garlic, minced
- 1 zucchini, diced
- 1 red bell pepper, diced
- 1 yellow bell pepper, diced
- 1 cup corn kernels (fresh or frozen)
- 1 can (14 oz) fire-roasted diced tomatoes, undrained
- 4 cups vegetable broth
- 1 teaspoon ground cumin
- 1 teaspoon chili powder
- 1/2 teaspoon smoked paprika
- Salt and pepper to taste
- 4 corn tortillas, cut into thin strips
- Optional garnishes: sliced avocado, chopped fresh cilantro, lime wedges

Instructions:

1. Preheat your oven to 425°F (220°C). Place the diced zucchini, red bell pepper, and yellow bell pepper on a baking sheet. Drizzle with olive oil, and season with salt and pepper. Toss to coat the vegetables evenly. Roast in the oven for about 20 minutes, or until the vegetables are tender and slightly charred.
2. In a large pot, heat the olive oil over medium heat. Add the chopped onion and minced garlic. Sauté until the onion becomes translucent.
3. Stir in the diced tomatoes, vegetable broth, ground cumin, chili powder, smoked paprika, salt, and pepper. Bring the mixture

to a boil, then reduce the heat and let it simmer for about 10 minutes.

4. Add the roasted vegetables and corn kernels to the pot. Simmer for an additional 5 minutes to allow the flavors to meld together.

5. While the soup is simmering, prepare the tortilla strips. Preheat your oven to 375°F (190°C). Place the tortilla strips on a baking sheet and bake for 8-10 minutes, or until they are crispy and golden brown.

6. Ladle the roasted vegetable tortilla soup into bowls. Top each bowl with a handful of crispy tortilla strips and any optional garnishes you desire, such as sliced avocado, chopped fresh cilantro, or lime wedges.

7. Serve the soup hot and enjoy the satisfying combination of roasted vegetables and warm spices in this plant-based tortilla soup.

With these vegan and plant-based tortilla soup recipes, you can explore the abundance of flavors that come from wholesome ingredients. From the smoky richness of black beans to the roasted goodness of vegetables, these recipes offer a delicious and nourishing twist on the classic tortilla soup. Embrace the plant-powered goodness and savor the vibrant flavors that these recipes have to offer.

Chapter 10: Hearty and Filling Tortilla Soup Bowls

In this chapter, we'll explore nourishing and substantial tortilla soup recipes that are perfect as main courses. These recipes go beyond the traditional soup and transform into hearty bowls packed with proteins, grains, and legumes. Prepare to indulge in satisfying meals that will keep you full and satisfied.

10.1 Chicken and Quinoa Tortilla Soup Bowl
Recipe: Chicken and Quinoa Tortilla Soup Bowl
Ingredients:

- 1 tablespoon olive oil
- 1 onion, chopped
- 3 cloves garlic, minced
- 1 red bell pepper, chopped
- 1 jalapeño pepper, seeded and finely chopped
- 1 teaspoon ground cumin
- 1 teaspoon chili powder
- 4 cups chicken broth
- 1 can (14 oz) diced tomatoes, undrained
- 1 cup cooked quinoa
- 2 cups cooked chicken breast, shredded
- 1 can (15 oz) black beans, drained and rinsed
- Salt and pepper to taste
- 4 corn tortillas, cut into thin strips
- Optional garnishes: sliced avocado, shredded cheese, chopped fresh cilantro, lime wedges

Instructions:

1. Heat the olive oil in a large pot over medium heat. Add the

chopped onion, minced garlic, red bell pepper, and jalapeño pepper. Sauté until the vegetables are tender.

2. Stir in the ground cumin and chili powder. Cook for another minute to toast the spices and release their flavors.

3. Add the chicken broth and diced tomatoes to the pot. Bring the mixture to a boil, then reduce the heat and let it simmer for about 10 minutes.

4. Stir in the cooked quinoa, shredded chicken breast, and black beans. Simmer for an additional 5 minutes to heat through.

5. Season with salt and pepper to taste. Adjust the seasonings according to your preference.

6. While the soup is simmering, prepare the tortilla strips. Preheat your oven to 375°F (190°C). Place the tortilla strips on a baking sheet and bake for 8-10 minutes, or until they are crispy and golden brown.

7. Ladle the chicken and quinoa tortilla soup into bowls. Top each bowl with a handful of crispy tortilla strips and any optional garnishes you desire, such as sliced avocado, shredded cheese, chopped fresh cilantro, or lime wedges.

8. Serve the soup hot and relish the heartiness and flavors of this satisfying tortilla soup bowl.

10.2 Vegan Lentil and Brown Rice Tortilla Soup Bowl
Recipe: Vegan Lentil and Brown Rice Tortilla Soup Bowl
Ingredients:

- 1 tablespoon olive oil
- 1 onion, chopped
- 3 cloves garlic, minced
- 1 red bell pepper, chopped
- 1 jalapeño pepper, seeded and finely chopped
- 1 teaspoon ground cumin
- 1 teaspoon chili powder
- 4 cups vegetable broth
- 1 can (14 oz) diced tomatoes, undrained
- 1/2 cup brown lentils, rinsed
- 1/2 cup cooked brown rice
- 1 can (15 oz) black beans, drained and rinsed
- Salt and pepper to taste
- 4 corn tortillas, cut into thin strips
- Optional garnishes: sliced avocado, chopped fresh cilantro, lime wedges

Instructions:

1. Heat the olive oil in a large pot over medium heat. Add the chopped onion, minced garlic, red bell pepper, and jalapeño pepper. Sauté until the vegetables are tender.
2. Stir in the ground cumin and chili powder. Cook for another minute to toast the spices and release their flavors.
3. Add the vegetable broth and diced tomatoes to the pot. Bring the mixture to a boil, then reduce the heat and let it simmer for about 10 minutes.
4. Stir in the brown lentils, cooked brown rice, and black beans. Simmer for an additional 15-20 minutes, or until the lentils are

tender.

5. Season with salt and pepper to taste. Adjust the seasonings according to your preference.

6. While the soup is simmering, prepare the tortilla strips. Preheat your oven to 375°F (190°C). Place the tortilla strips on a baking sheet and bake for 8-10 minutes, or until they are crispy and golden brown.

7. Ladle the lentil and brown rice tortilla soup into bowls. Top each bowl with a handful of crispy tortilla strips and any optional garnishes you desire, such as sliced avocado, chopped fresh cilantro, or lime wedges.

8. Serve the soup hot and enjoy the wholesome combination of lentils, brown rice, and vegetables in this hearty vegan tortilla soup bowl.

These hearty and filling tortilla soup bowls take the classic dish to a whole new level by incorporating proteins, grains, and legumes. Whether you choose the chicken and quinoa option or the vegan lentil and brown rice version, these recipes are sure to satisfy your appetite and provide a well-rounded meal in a single bowl. Enjoy the nourishment and flavors as you savor each spoonful.

Chapter 11: Comforting Tortilla Soup for the Soul

In this chapter, we'll explore soul-warming tortilla soup recipes that are perfect for cozy evenings. These recipes are designed to evoke feelings of comfort and nostalgia, transporting you to a place of warmth and contentment. Get ready to indulge in bowls of soup that will soothe your soul and bring a smile to your face.

11.1 Grandma's Chicken Tortilla Soup
Recipe: Grandma's Chicken Tortilla Soup
Ingredients:

- 1 whole chicken, cut into pieces
- 1 onion, chopped
- 3 cloves garlic, minced
- 2 carrots, diced
- 2 stalks celery, diced
- 1 jalapeño pepper, seeded and finely chopped
- 1 teaspoon ground cumin
- 1 teaspoon dried oregano
- 1 bay leaf
- Salt and pepper to taste
- 8 cups chicken broth
- 1 can (14 oz) diced tomatoes, undrained
- 1 cup corn kernels (fresh or frozen)
- 4 corn tortillas, cut into thin strips
- Optional garnishes: sliced avocado, chopped fresh cilantro, lime wedges

Instructions:

1. In a large pot, add the chicken pieces, chopped onion, minced

garlic, diced carrots, diced celery, jalapeño pepper, ground cumin, dried oregano, bay leaf, salt, and pepper.

2. Pour in the chicken broth and diced tomatoes with their juice. Bring the mixture to a boil, then reduce the heat and let it simmer for about 45 minutes, or until the chicken is cooked through and tender.

3. Remove the chicken pieces from the pot and set them aside to cool. Once cooled, shred the chicken into bite-sized pieces and discard the bones.

4. Return the shredded chicken to the pot. Add the corn kernels and let the soup simmer for another 15 minutes to allow the flavors to meld together.

5. While the soup is simmering, prepare the tortilla strips. Preheat your oven to 375°F (190°C). Place the tortilla strips on a baking sheet and bake for 8-10 minutes, or until they are crispy and golden brown.

6. Ladle the Grandma's chicken tortilla soup into bowls. Top each bowl with a handful of crispy tortilla strips and any optional garnishes you desire, such as sliced avocado, chopped fresh cilantro, or lime wedges.

7. Serve the soup hot and savor the comforting flavors and memories that this soup brings. It's like a warm hug from Grandma in a bowl.

11.2 Homestyle Beef Tortilla Soup
Recipe: Homestyle Beef Tortilla Soup
Ingredients:

- 1 pound beef stew meat, cubed
- 1 onion, chopped
- 3 cloves garlic, minced
- 1 red bell pepper, chopped
- 1 jalapeño pepper, seeded and finely chopped
- 1 teaspoon ground cumin
- 1 teaspoon chili powder
- Salt and pepper to taste
- 8 cups beef broth
- 1 can (14 oz) diced tomatoes, undrained
- 1 cup corn kernels (fresh or frozen)
- 4 corn tortillas, cut into thin strips
- Optional garnishes: shredded cheese, chopped fresh cilantro, lime wedges

Instructions:

1. In a large pot, heat some oil over medium heat. Add the beef stew meat and cook until browned on all sides. Remove the beef from the pot and set it aside.
2. In the same pot, add the chopped onion, minced garlic, chopped red bell pepper, and jalapeño pepper. Sauté until the vegetables are tender and aromatic.
3. Return the browned beef to the pot. Stir in the ground cumin, chili powder, salt, and pepper. Cook for another minute to coat the beef and vegetables with the spices.
4. Pour in the beef broth and diced tomatoes with their juice. Bring the mixture to a boil, then reduce the heat and let it simmer for about 1 hour, or until the beef is tender.

5. Add the corn kernels to the pot and let the soup simmer for another 15 minutes to allow the flavors to meld together.

6. While the soup is simmering, prepare the tortilla strips. Preheat your oven to 375°F (190°C). Place the tortilla strips on a baking sheet and bake for 8-10 minutes, or until they are crispy and golden brown.

7. Ladle the Homestyle beef tortilla soup into bowls. Top each bowl with a handful of crispy tortilla strips and any optional garnishes you desire, such as shredded cheese, chopped fresh cilantro, or lime wedges.

8. Serve the soup hot and enjoy the comforting flavors and heartiness of this homestyle beef tortilla soup.

These comforting tortilla soup recipes are like a warm embrace on a chilly evening. Whether you choose the nostalgic flavors of Grandma's chicken tortilla soup or the homestyle goodness of beef tortilla soup, each spoonful will transport you to a place of comfort and contentment. Sit back, relax, and savor the soul-warming deliciousness.

Chapter 12: Fresh and Vibrant Tortilla Soup Salads

In this chapter, we'll explore innovative twists on tortilla soup with a salad-inspired approach. These recipes combine the flavors and elements of tortilla soup with the light and refreshing qualities of a salad. Get ready to indulge in fresh and vibrant tortilla soup salads that are perfect for a light and satisfying meal.

12.1 Grilled Chicken Tortilla Soup Salad
Recipe: Grilled Chicken Tortilla Soup Salad
Ingredients:

- 1-pound boneless, skinless chicken breasts
- 1 teaspoon chili powder
- 1 teaspoon ground cumin
- Salt and pepper to taste
- 4 cups mixed salad greens
- 1 cup cherry tomatoes, halved
- 1 avocado, sliced
- 1/4 cup diced red onion
- 1/4 cup sliced black olives
- 1/4 cup chopped fresh cilantro
- 1 lime, cut into wedges
- Tortilla strips for garnish

For the dressing:

- 1/4 cup olive oil
- 2 tablespoons lime juice
- 1 tablespoon honey
- 1 clove garlic, minced

- Salt and pepper to taste

Instructions:

1. Preheat your grill or grill pan over medium-high heat.
2. Season the chicken breasts with chili powder, ground cumin, salt, and pepper. Grill the chicken for about 6-8 minutes per side, or until cooked through. Remove from the grill and let it rest for a few minutes. Slice the chicken into thin strips.
3. In a large bowl, combine the mixed salad greens, cherry tomatoes, avocado slices, diced red onion, sliced black olives, and chopped fresh cilantro.
4. In a small bowl, whisk together the olive oil, lime juice, honey, minced garlic, salt, and pepper to make the dressing.
5. Drizzle the dressing over the salad and toss to coat the ingredients evenly.
6. Divide the salad among serving plates. Top each plate with the grilled chicken strips and a handful of tortilla strips for garnish.
7. Serve the grilled chicken tortilla soup salad with lime wedges on the side for squeezing over the salad.

12.2 Shrimp and Corn Tortilla Soup Salad
Recipe: Shrimp and Corn Tortilla Soup Salad
Ingredients:

- 1-pound medium shrimp, peeled and deveined
- 1 teaspoon chili powder
- 1 teaspoon smoked paprika
- Salt and pepper to taste
- 4 cups mixed salad greens
- 1 cup corn kernels (fresh or frozen)
- 1/2 cup diced red bell pepper
- 1/4 cup diced red onion
- 1/4 cup chopped fresh cilantro
- 1 lime, cut into wedges
- Tortilla strips for garnish

For the dressing:

- 1/4 cup olive oil
- 2 tablespoons lime juice
- 1 tablespoon honey
- 1 clove garlic, minced
- Salt and pepper to taste

Instructions:

1. Preheat a grill or grill pan over medium-high heat.
2. Season the shrimp with chili powder, smoked paprika, salt, and pepper. Grill the shrimp for about 2-3 minutes per side, or until pink and cooked through. Remove from the grill.
3. In a large bowl, combine the mixed salad greens, corn kernels, diced red bell pepper, diced red onion, and chopped fresh

cilantro.

4. In a small bowl, whisk together the olive oil, lime juice, honey, minced garlic, salt, and pepper to make the dressing.
5. Drizzle the dressing over the salad and toss to coat the ingredients evenly.
6. Divide the salad among serving plates. Top each plate with the grilled shrimp and a handful of tortilla strips for garnish.
7. Serve the shrimp and corn tortilla soup salad with lime wedges on the side for squeezing over the salad.

These fresh and vibrant tortilla soup salads are a delightful combination of flavors and textures. Whether you choose the grilled chicken version or the shrimp and corn option, each salad brings together the best of tortilla soup and refreshing salad ingredients. Enjoy the lightness and vibrancy of these unique creations.

Chapter 13: Exotic and Unique Tortilla Soup Infusions

In this chapter, we'll dive into the world of adventurous combinations of ingredients that will elevate your tortilla soup experience to a whole new level. Prepare yourself for unexpected flavors and unique ingredients that will tantalize your taste buds and leave you craving more. Get ready for a culinary adventure with these exotic and innovative tortilla soup infusions.

13.1 Thai Curry Tortilla Soup
Recipe: Thai Curry Tortilla Soup
Ingredients:

- 1 tablespoon vegetable oil
- 1 onion, chopped
- 3 cloves garlic, minced
- 1 tablespoon Thai red curry paste
- 1 can (14 oz) coconut milk
- 4 cups chicken or vegetable broth
- 1 cup diced tomatoes
- 1 cup diced bell peppers (assorted colors)
- 1 cup sliced mushrooms
- 1 cup diced zucchini
- 1 cup cooked chicken, shredded (optional)
- 1 tablespoon fish sauce (optional)
- Juice of 1 lime
- Salt and pepper to taste
- Fresh cilantro, chopped, for garnish
- Tortilla strips, for garnish

Instructions:

1. Heat the vegetable oil in a large pot over medium heat. Add the chopped onion and minced garlic, and sauté until fragrant and softened.
2. Stir in the Thai red curry paste and cook for another minute to release its flavors.
3. Pour in the coconut milk and chicken or vegetable broth. Stir well to combine.
4. Add the diced tomatoes, bell peppers, mushrooms, and zucchini to the pot. If desired, add cooked chicken for added protein and flavor. Stir to combine.
5. Bring the soup to a simmer and let it cook for about 15-20 minutes, or until the vegetables are tender.
6. Stir in the fish sauce, if using, and the lime juice. Season with salt and pepper to taste.
7. Ladle the Thai curry tortilla soup into bowls. Garnish each bowl with fresh cilantro and a handful of tortilla strips for added crunch and texture.
8. Serve the soup hot and immerse yourself in the exotic flavors and fragrant aromas of this unique tortilla soup infusion.

13.2 Mediterranean-Inspired Tortilla Soup
Recipe: Mediterranean-Inspired Tortilla Soup
Ingredients:

- 1 tablespoon olive oil
- 1 onion, chopped
- 3 cloves garlic, minced
- 1 teaspoon ground cumin
- 1 teaspoon dried oregano
- 1 can (14 oz) diced tomatoes
- 4 cups chicken or vegetable broth
- 1 cup canned chickpeas, rinsed and drained
- 1 cup sliced black olives
- 1 cup chopped roasted red peppers
- 1 cup chopped spinach or kale
- Juice of 1 lemon
- Salt and pepper to taste
- Crumbled feta cheese, for garnish
- Fresh parsley, chopped, for garnish
- Tortilla strips, for garnish

Instructions:

1. Heat the olive oil in a large pot over medium heat. Add the chopped onion and minced garlic, and sauté until fragrant and translucent.
2. Stir in the ground cumin and dried oregano, and cook for another minute to toast the spices.
3. Add the diced tomatoes, chicken or vegetable broth, chickpeas, black olives, roasted red peppers, and chopped spinach or kale to the pot. Stir well to combine.
4. Bring the soup to a simmer and let it cook for about 15 minutes to allow the flavors to meld together.

5. Stir in the lemon juice. Season with salt and pepper to taste.

6. Ladle the Mediterranean-inspired tortilla soup into bowls. Garnish each bowl with crumbled feta cheese, fresh parsley, and a handful of tortilla strips for added texture and visual appeal.

7. Serve the soup hot and savor the delightful blend of Mediterranean flavors in this unique tortilla soup infusion.

Get ready to embark on a culinary adventure with these exotic and unique tortilla soup infusions. The Thai Curry Tortilla Soup will transport you to the vibrant streets of Thailand with its aromatic spices and creamy coconut milk base. On the other hand, the Mediterranean-Inspired Tortilla Soup will take you on a journey through the flavors of the Mediterranean with its blend of herbs, roasted red peppers, and tangy feta cheese. Expand your palate and embrace the unexpected with these extraordinary tortilla soup creations.

Chapter 14: Quick and Easy Tortilla Soup Recipes

In this chapter, we'll explore time-saving recipes for those busy days when you're in a hurry but still crave a delicious bowl of tortilla soup. These recipes are designed to be simple yet packed with flavor, allowing you to enjoy a satisfying meal without spending hours in the kitchen. Let's dive into these quick and easy tortilla soup variations that are perfect for busy individuals.

14.1 30-Minute Tortilla Soup
Recipe: 30-Minute Tortilla Soup
Ingredients:

- 1 tablespoon olive oil
- 1 onion, diced
- 3 cloves garlic, minced
- 1 teaspoon ground cumin
- 1 teaspoon chili powder
- 1 can (14 oz) diced tomatoes
- 4 cups chicken or vegetable broth
- 1 cup frozen corn kernels
- 1 cup cooked shredded chicken
- Juice of 1 lime
- Salt and pepper to taste
- Tortilla chips, for garnish
- Fresh cilantro, chopped, for garnish
- Lime wedges, for serving

Instructions:

1. Heat the olive oil in a large pot over medium heat. Add the diced onion and minced garlic, and sauté until softened and

fragrant.

2. Stir in the ground cumin and chili powder, and cook for another minute to toast the spices.
3. Add the diced tomatoes (with their juice), chicken or vegetable broth, frozen corn kernels, and cooked shredded chicken to the pot. Stir well to combine.
4. Bring the soup to a boil, then reduce the heat and let it simmer for about 15 minutes to allow the flavors to meld together.
5. Stir in the lime juice. Season with salt and pepper to taste.
6. Ladle the 30-Minute Tortilla Soup into bowls. Garnish each bowl with a handful of tortilla chips, fresh cilantro, and a lime wedge on the side.
7. Serve the soup hot and enjoy the quick and satisfying flavors of this easy tortilla soup recipe.

14.2 One-Pot Tortilla Soup
Recipe: One-Pot Tortilla Soup
Ingredients:

- 1 tablespoon vegetable oil
- 1 onion, chopped
- 2 cloves garlic, minced
- 1 bell pepper, diced
- 1 can (14 oz) black beans, rinsed and drained
- 1 can (14 oz) diced tomatoes
- 4 cups chicken or vegetable broth
- 1 teaspoon ground cumin
- 1 teaspoon chili powder
- Salt and pepper to taste
- Tortilla strips, for garnish
- Shredded cheese, for garnish
- Avocado slices, for garnish

Instructions:

1. In a large pot, heat the vegetable oil over medium heat. Add the chopped onion, minced garlic, and diced bell pepper. Sauté until the vegetables are softened and fragrant.
2. Add the black beans (rinsed and drained), diced tomatoes (with their juice), chicken or vegetable broth, ground cumin, and chili powder to the pot. Stir well to combine.
3. Bring the soup to a boil, then reduce the heat and let it simmer for about 20 minutes, or until the flavors have melded together.
4. Season the soup with salt and pepper to taste.
5. Ladle the One-Pot Tortilla Soup into bowls. Garnish each bowl with a handful of tortilla strips, shredded cheese, and avocado slices.
6. Serve the soup hot and revel in the simplicity and deliciousness

of this one-pot tortilla soup recipe.

These quick and easy tortilla soup recipes are perfect for those times when you need a satisfying meal in a hurry. The 30-Minute Tortilla Soup is packed with flavorful ingredients and comes together in just half an hour, making it a perfect option for busy weeknights. Meanwhile, the One-Pot Tortilla Soup simplifies the cooking process by utilizing just one pot, minimizing cleanup while still delivering delicious results. Enjoy the convenience and deliciousness of these quick and easy tortilla soup variations.

Chapter 15: Creative Tortilla Soup Appetizers

In this chapter, we'll explore bite-sized tortilla soup creations that are perfect for parties, gatherings, or any occasion where you want to impress your guests. These miniature cups, shooters, and finger foods offer a delightful way to enjoy the flavors of tortilla soup in a convenient and appetizing format. Get ready to wow your guests with these creative tortilla soup appetizers.

15.1 Tortilla Soup Shooters
Recipe: Tortilla Soup Shooters
Ingredients:

- 1 batch of your favorite tortilla soup (choose one from the previous chapters)
- Small shot glasses or shooter glasses
- Tortilla strips, for garnish
- Fresh cilantro, chopped, for garnish
- Lime wedges, for serving

Instructions:

1. Prepare a batch of your favorite tortilla soup according to the recipe of your choice.
2. Allow the soup to cool slightly before assembling the shooters.
3. Pour the tortilla soup into small shot glasses or shooter glasses, filling them about three-quarters of the way.
4. Garnish each shooter with a few tortilla strips and a sprinkle of fresh cilantro.
5. Serve the tortilla soup shooters with lime wedges on the side for squeezing over the soup.
6. Your guests can simply pick up a shooter glass and sip on the

flavorful tortilla soup, enjoying the vibrant flavors in a convenient and fun way.

15.2 Miniature Tortilla Soup Cups
Recipe: Miniature Tortilla Soup Cups
Ingredients:

- Small tortilla cups (store-bought or homemade)
- 1 batch of your favorite tortilla soup (choose one from the previous chapters)
- Shredded cheese, for topping
- Diced avocado, for topping
- Fresh cilantro, chopped, for garnish

Instructions:

1. Preheat your oven according to the instructions on the tortilla cup packaging if using store-bought cups. If making homemade tortilla cups, follow your chosen recipe.
2. Once the tortilla cups are ready, fill each cup with a spoonful of your favorite tortilla soup.
3. Top each cup with a sprinkle of shredded cheese and diced avocado.
4. Place the filled cups on a baking sheet and bake them in the preheated oven for a few minutes, or until the cheese has melted and the cups are heated through.
5. Remove the cups from the oven and garnish with fresh cilantro.
6. Arrange the miniature tortilla soup cups on a serving platter and watch as your guests enjoy these adorable and delicious bite-sized treats.

These creative tortilla soup appetizers are sure to impress your guests with their unique presentation and delicious flavors. Whether you opt for the Tortilla Soup Shooters or the Miniature Tortilla Soup Cups, you'll be offering a delightful way to savor the essence of tortilla soup in a bite-sized format. Enjoy these creative appetizers at your next gathering and delight your guests with the flavors of tortilla soup in a fun and appetizing way.

Chapter 16: Tortilla Soup Inspired Sides and Accompaniments

In this chapter, we'll explore complementary dishes and sides that perfectly pair with tortilla soup, enhancing the overall dining experience. These flavorful accompaniments will elevate your tortilla soup to new heights, providing a variety of textures and flavors to delight your taste buds. From homemade tortilla chips to zesty salsa and creamy guacamole, get ready to discover the perfect sides to serve alongside your tortilla soup.

16.1 Homemade Tortilla Chips

Recipe: Homemade Tortilla Chips

Ingredients:

- Corn tortillas
- Vegetable oil, for frying
- Salt, to taste

Instructions:

1. Cut the corn tortillas into triangles or desired shapes.
2. In a large skillet or frying pan, heat vegetable oil over medium heat.
3. Once the oil is hot, carefully add the tortilla triangles in batches, making sure not to overcrowd the pan.
4. Fry the tortilla chips until golden brown and crispy, flipping them occasionally to ensure even frying.
5. Use a slotted spoon or tongs to remove the chips from the oil and transfer them to a paper towel-lined plate to drain excess oil.
6. While the chips are still warm, sprinkle them with salt to taste.
7. Allow the chips to cool completely before serving. They will

continue to crisp up as they cool.

16.2 Zesty Salsa
Recipe: Zesty Salsa
Ingredients:

- 3 large tomatoes, diced
- 1 small onion, finely chopped
- 1 jalapeno pepper, seeds removed and finely chopped
- 1/4 cup fresh cilantro, chopped
- Juice of 1 lime
- Salt and pepper, to taste

Instructions:

1. In a mixing bowl, combine the diced tomatoes, chopped onion, jalapeno pepper, and fresh cilantro.
2. Squeeze the lime juice over the mixture and season with salt and pepper.
3. Stir everything together until well combined.
4. Allow the salsa to sit for at least 15 minutes to allow the flavors to meld together.
5. Taste and adjust the seasoning if needed.
6. Serve the zesty salsa alongside your tortilla soup, allowing your guests to add a spoonful or two to their bowls for an extra burst of freshness and tanginess.

16.3 Creamy Guacamole
Recipe: Creamy Guacamole
Ingredients:

- 2 ripe avocados
- 1 small tomato, diced
- 1/4 cup red onion, finely chopped
- 1/4 cup fresh cilantro, chopped
- Juice of 1 lime
- Salt and pepper, to taste

Instructions:

1. Cut the avocados in half, remove the pits, and scoop out the flesh into a mixing bowl.
2. Mash the avocado flesh with a fork until smooth, or leave it slightly chunky if desired.
3. Add the diced tomato, finely chopped red onion, and fresh cilantro to the mashed avocado.
4. Squeeze the lime juice over the mixture and season with salt and pepper.
5. Stir everything together until well combined.
6. Taste and adjust the seasoning if needed.
7. Cover the guacamole with plastic wrap, ensuring the wrap touches the surface to prevent browning.
8. Refrigerate for at least 30 minutes to allow the flavors to meld together.
9. Serve the creamy guacamole alongside your tortilla soup, offering a dollop or two on top of each bowl for a creamy and refreshing contrast.

These tortilla soup inspired sides and accompaniments will enhance the overall dining experience, adding extra crunch, zest, and creaminess to complement the flavors of the soup. Whether you're enjoying homemade tortilla chips, zesty salsa, or creamy guacamole, these delicious additions will take your tortilla soup to the next level. Serve them alongside your soup, allowing your guests to customize their bowls with their preferred sides and accompaniments. Enjoy the perfect combination of flavors and textures with these tortilla soup inspired accompaniments.

Chapter 17: Family-Friendly Tortilla Soup Recipes

In this chapter, we'll explore kid-approved tortilla soup recipes with mild flavors that the whole family can enjoy. These recipes are designed to be flavorful yet approachable for younger palates, ensuring that everyone at the table can savor a delicious bowl of tortilla soup together. Let's dive into these family-friendly tortilla soup recipes and create memorable meals for your loved ones.

17.1 Mild Chicken Tortilla Soup
Recipe: Mild Chicken Tortilla Soup
Ingredients:

- 1 tablespoon vegetable oil
- 1 onion, diced
- 2 cloves garlic, minced
- 1 bell pepper, diced
- 1 carrot, diced
- 2 cups cooked shredded chicken
- 4 cups chicken broth
- 1 can (14 oz) diced tomatoes
- 1 teaspoon ground cumin
- 1 teaspoon chili powder
- Salt and pepper, to taste
- Tortilla strips, for garnish
- Shredded cheese, for garnish
- Sour cream, for garnish
- Fresh cilantro, chopped, for garnish

Instructions:

1. In a large pot, heat the vegetable oil over medium heat. Add the

diced onion, minced garlic, diced bell pepper, and diced carrot. Sauté until the vegetables are softened.

2. Add the cooked shredded chicken, chicken broth, diced tomatoes (with their juice), ground cumin, and chili powder to the pot. Stir well to combine.

3. Bring the soup to a boil, then reduce the heat and let it simmer for about 15 minutes to allow the flavors to meld together.

4. Season the soup with salt and pepper to taste.

5. Ladle the Mild Chicken Tortilla Soup into bowls. Garnish each bowl with a handful of tortilla strips, shredded cheese, a dollop of sour cream, and a sprinkle of fresh cilantro.

6. Serve the soup hot and enjoy the comforting flavors of this mild and family-friendly tortilla soup.

17.2 Vegetable Tortilla Soup
Recipe: Vegetable Tortilla Soup
Ingredients:

- 1 tablespoon olive oil
- 1 onion, diced
- 2 cloves garlic, minced
- 1 zucchini, diced
- 1 yellow squash, diced
- 1 bell pepper, diced
- 1 can (14 oz) diced tomatoes
- 4 cups vegetable broth
- 1 teaspoon ground cumin
- 1 teaspoon chili powder
- Salt and pepper, to taste
- Tortilla strips, for garnish
- Fresh cilantro, chopped, for garnish
- Lime wedges, for serving

Instructions:

1. In a large pot, heat the olive oil over medium heat. Add the diced onion and minced garlic, and sauté until the vegetables are softened.
2. Add the diced zucchini, yellow squash, bell pepper, diced tomatoes (with their juice), vegetable broth, ground cumin, and chili powder to the pot. Stir well to combine.
3. Bring the soup to a boil, then reduce the heat and let it simmer for about 15 minutes, or until the vegetables are tender.
4. Season the soup with salt and pepper to taste.
5. Ladle the Vegetable Tortilla Soup into bowls. Garnish each bowl with a handful of tortilla strips and a sprinkle of fresh cilantro.

6. Serve the soup hot and squeeze fresh lime juice over each bowl for a burst of citrusy freshness.
7. Enjoy the vibrant flavors of this vegetable-packed tortilla soup that the whole family will love.

These family-friendly tortilla soup recipes are sure to please even the pickiest eaters. The Mild Chicken Tortilla Soup offers a comforting blend of flavors with tender chicken, while the Vegetable Tortilla Soup showcases a medley of colorful and nutritious vegetables. Gather your family around the table and enjoy these delicious and approachable tortilla soups together.

Chapter 18: Brunch and Breakfast Tortilla Soup Ideas

In this chapter, we'll explore unique ways to incorporate tortilla soup into morning meals, creating delicious brunch and breakfast options that will awaken your taste buds. From egg-based recipes to breakfast-inspired twists, these creative dishes will transform your tortilla soup into a delightful morning indulgence. Get ready to start your day with a flavorful and satisfying breakfast twist on tortilla soup.

18.1 Huevos Rancheros Tortilla Soup

Recipe: Huevos Rancheros Tortilla Soup

Ingredients:

- 1 tablespoon vegetable oil
- 1 onion, diced
- 2 cloves garlic, minced
- 1 bell pepper, diced
- 1 jalapeno pepper, seeds removed and finely chopped
- 1 can (14 oz) diced tomatoes
- 4 cups chicken or vegetable broth
- 1 teaspoon ground cumin
- 1 teaspoon chili powder
- Salt and pepper, to taste
- Eggs (1-2 per serving)
- Tortilla strips, for garnish
- Fresh cilantro, chopped, for garnish
- Lime wedges, for serving

Instructions:

1. In a large pot, heat the vegetable oil over medium heat. Add the diced onion, minced garlic, diced bell pepper, and chopped

jalapeno pepper. Sauté until the vegetables are softened.

2. Add the diced tomatoes (with their juice), chicken or vegetable broth, ground cumin, and chili powder to the pot. Stir well to combine.

3. Bring the soup to a boil, then reduce the heat and let it simmer for about 15 minutes to allow the flavors to meld together.

4. Season the soup with salt and pepper to taste.

5. While the soup is simmering, prepare the eggs. You can either poach the eggs directly in the soup or cook them separately according to your preference.

6. To serve, ladle the Huevos Rancheros Tortilla Soup into bowls. Top each bowl with a poached egg or a cooked egg of your choice.

7. Garnish each bowl with a handful of tortilla strips, a sprinkle of fresh cilantro, and a squeeze of fresh lime juice.

8. Serve the soup hot and enjoy the combination of rich flavors from the tortilla soup and the luscious eggs for a brunch delight.

18.2 Breakfast Tortilla Soup Bowl
Recipe: Breakfast Tortilla Soup Bowl
Ingredients:

- 1 tablespoon vegetable oil
- 1 onion, diced
- 2 cloves garlic, minced
- 1 bell pepper, diced
- 1 jalapeno pepper, seeds removed and finely chopped
- 1 can (14 oz) diced tomatoes
- 4 cups chicken or vegetable broth
- 1 teaspoon ground cumin
- 1 teaspoon chili powder
- Salt and pepper, to taste
- Cooked breakfast sausage or bacon, crumbled
- Cooked hash browns or diced potatoes
- Scrambled eggs
- Shredded cheese, for garnish
- Avocado slices, for garnish
- Fresh cilantro, chopped, for garnish

Instructions:

1. In a large pot, heat the vegetable oil over medium heat. Add the diced onion, minced garlic, diced bell pepper, and chopped jalapeno pepper. Sauté until the vegetables are softened.
2. Add the diced tomatoes (with their juice), chicken or vegetable broth, ground cumin, and chili powder to the pot. Stir well to combine.
3. Bring the soup to a boil, then reduce the heat and let it simmer for about 15 minutes to allow the flavors to meld together.
4. Season the soup with salt and pepper to taste.
5. While the soup is simmering, prepare the breakfast ingredients.

Cook the breakfast sausage or bacon, crumble it into pieces. Cook the hash browns or diced potatoes until crispy. Scramble the eggs.

6. To serve, ladle the Breakfast Tortilla Soup into bowls. Top each bowl with a portion of cooked sausage or bacon, a scoop of crispy hash browns or diced potatoes, and a serving of scrambled eggs.

7. Garnish each bowl with a sprinkle of shredded cheese, a few avocado slices, and a sprinkle of fresh cilantro.

8. Serve the soup hot and savor the delightful combination of breakfast flavors in a unique tortilla soup bowl.

These brunch and breakfast tortilla soup ideas will add a delightful twist to your morning routine. Whether you choose the Huevos Rancheros Tortilla Soup with its poached eggs or the Breakfast Tortilla Soup Bowl with a hearty breakfast combination, these recipes will surely wake up your taste buds and provide a satisfying start to your day.

Chapter 19: Sweet Endings with Tortilla Soup Desserts

In this chapter, we'll explore unexpected and creative dessert recipes that incorporate tortilla soup as a unique and flavorful ingredient. From sweet soups to ice cream and tortilla-based treats, these dessert creations will leave you with a sweet ending to your meal. Prepare to indulge in the delightful combination of sweet flavors and the comforting essence of tortilla soup.

19.1 Chocolate Tortilla Soup
Recipe: Chocolate Tortilla Soup
Ingredients:

- 4 cups milk
- 2 cups chocolate chips (dark, milk, or a combination)
- 1/4 cup sugar
- 1 teaspoon vanilla extract
- 1/4 teaspoon ground cinnamon
- Pinch of salt
- Tortilla strips or crushed tortilla chips, for garnish
- Whipped cream, for garnish
- Fresh berries, for garnish

Instructions:

1. In a saucepan, heat the milk over medium heat until it starts to simmer.
2. Add the chocolate chips, sugar, vanilla extract, ground cinnamon, and pinch of salt to the saucepan. Stir continuously until the chocolate chips have melted and the mixture is smooth and well combined.
3. Remove the saucepan from heat and let the chocolate soup cool slightly.
4. Once cooled, transfer the chocolate soup to serving bowls.
5. Garnish each bowl with a handful of tortilla strips or crushed tortilla chips, a dollop of whipped cream, and a sprinkle of fresh berries.
6. Serve the Chocolate Tortilla Soup warm or chilled and enjoy the rich and indulgent flavors of this unique dessert.

19.2 Cinnamon Sugar Tortilla Chips with Fruit Salsa
Recipe: Cinnamon Sugar Tortilla Chips with Fruit Salsa
Ingredients:

- Flour tortillas
- Butter, melted
- Cinnamon sugar mixture (1/4 cup sugar + 1 teaspoon ground cinnamon)
- Assorted fresh fruits (strawberries, pineapple, mango, etc.), diced
- Fresh mint leaves, chopped
- Lime juice, for drizzling

Instructions:

1. Preheat the oven to 350°F (175°C).
2. Brush both sides of the flour tortillas with melted butter.
3. Sprinkle the cinnamon sugar mixture evenly over the buttered tortillas.
4. Stack the tortillas and cut them into desired chip shapes (triangles, squares, or circles).
5. Place the cinnamon sugar-coated tortilla chips on a baking sheet and bake in the preheated oven for about 10-12 minutes, or until crispy and golden brown.
6. While the tortilla chips are baking, prepare the fruit salsa. In a bowl, combine the diced fresh fruits, chopped mint leaves, and a drizzle of lime juice. Toss gently to mix.
7. Remove the tortilla chips from the oven and let them cool slightly.
8. Serve the Cinnamon Sugar Tortilla Chips with the fruit salsa on the side for dipping or spooning over the chips.
9. Enjoy the combination of crispy, sweet tortilla chips and the refreshing flavors of the fruit salsa.

These sweet endings with tortilla soup desserts offer a unique twist to satisfy your sweet tooth. Whether you indulge in the creamy and rich Chocolate Tortilla Soup or enjoy the crunchy and sweet Cinnamon Sugar Tortilla Chips with Fruit Salsa, these desserts will provide a delightful conclusion to your meal with a touch of tortilla soup-inspired creativity.

Chapter 20: Mastering Tortilla Soup Techniques and Tips

In this final chapter, we'll delve into advanced techniques, troubleshoot common issues, and provide expert advice to help you become a master of tortilla soup. These tips and tricks will elevate your culinary skills, enhance flavors, improve presentation, and encourage experimentation with this beloved dish. Get ready to take your tortilla soup to the next level with these valuable insights.

20.1 Flavor Enhancements and Ingredient Substitutions

Experiment with different types of chili peppers to vary the heat and flavor profile of your tortilla soup. Try jalapenos, poblanos, or even chipotle peppers for a smoky twist.

Use homemade chicken or vegetable broth for a more flavorful base. Simmering bones, herbs, and vegetables together will result in a rich and aromatic broth.

Add depth to your soup by incorporating spices like cumin, paprika, coriander, or oregano. These spices can enhance the overall flavor profile.

Consider adding a splash of lime juice or a drizzle of vinegar just before serving to brighten the flavors of the soup.

Feel free to experiment with additional ingredients such as roasted corn, black beans, or diced avocado to add extra texture and flavor to your tortilla soup.

For a creamier texture, blend a portion of the soup or use an immersion blender to partially puree the ingredients while leaving some chunky bits for added texture.

20.2 Presentation Tips

Garnish your tortilla soup with fresh ingredients such as chopped cilantro, diced tomatoes, sliced jalapenos, or a sprinkle of crumbled cheese to add visual appeal and extra flavor.

Serve tortilla soup in colorful bowls or mugs to make the presentation more inviting and appealing.

Consider serving tortilla soup alongside a platter of garnishes, such as tortilla strips, sour cream, chopped green onions, or shredded cheese. This allows your guests to customize their soup to their liking.

Arrange tortilla strips or chips in a crisscross pattern on top of the soup for an attractive and crunchy garnish.

For an elegant touch, drizzle a swirl of crema or yogurt on top of the soup just before serving.

20.3 Troubleshooting Common Issues

If your tortilla soup is too thin, let it simmer uncovered for a longer period to reduce and thicken the liquid. Alternatively, you can mix a tablespoon of cornstarch with a little cold water and add it to the soup, then simmer until thickened.

If your tortilla soup is too thick, you can thin it out by adding a bit more broth or water until you achieve the desired consistency.

If your tortilla soup lacks flavor, try adding a pinch of salt or a squeeze of lime juice to enhance the overall taste. You can also let the soup simmer for a bit longer to allow the flavors to develop.

20.4 Embracing Experimentation

Don't be afraid to get creative and experiment with different ingredients, spices, and flavors in your tortilla soup. Feel free to adapt recipes to suit your taste preferences and dietary needs.

Try incorporating unique toppings like crumbled bacon, pickled onions, or toasted pumpkin seeds to add an extra layer of complexity to your soup.

Consider using different types of tortillas, such as corn or flour tortillas, to add a distinct texture and flavor to your soup.

Explore fusion-inspired combinations by incorporating elements from other cuisines, such as Thai-inspired tortilla soup with lemongrass and coconut milk or Indian-inspired tortilla soup with curry spices.

By mastering these tortilla soup techniques and tips, you'll be equipped to create delicious and visually appealing soups, troubleshoot common issues, and unleash your creativity in the kitchen. Whether you're a seasoned chef or an enthusiastic home cook, these insights will help you elevate your tortilla soup game and impress your family and friends with your culinary prowess. Enjoy the journey of mastering the art of tortilla soup!

Congratulations! You have completed your journey through the "Tortilla Soup Cookbook." From learning about the history and origins of tortilla soup to exploring a wide array of delicious recipes and innovative variations, you have gained the knowledge and skills to become a true tortilla soup connoisseur.

Throughout this cookbook, we have covered everything from classic tortilla soup recipes to creamy, spicy, healthy, seafood-inspired, and international variations. We have also delved into the world of slow cookers, Instant Pots, vegan options, hearty main courses, comforting options, refreshing salads, exotic infusions, quick and easy recipes, appetizers, side dishes, family-friendly options, brunch ideas, sweet desserts, and mastering techniques and tips.

You have learned to balance flavors, experiment with ingredients, troubleshoot common issues, and enhance the presentation of your tortilla soups. With each chapter, you have discovered new possibilities and unleashed your creativity in the kitchen.

Remember, tortilla soup is not just a dish; it is a canvas for culinary exploration. Feel free to mix and match ingredients, adapt recipes to your preferences, and embark on new flavor adventures. Let your imagination soar as you continue to innovate and create your own unique tortilla soup masterpieces.

We hope this cookbook has inspired you to continue your culinary journey and sparked a love for the diverse and delicious world of tortilla soup. So grab your apron, gather your ingredients, and get ready to delight your taste buds with the comforting and flavorful embrace of tortilla soup. Happy cooking and enjoy every spoonful of this beloved dish!

May your tortilla soups always be a source of joy, warmth, and shared memories with your loved ones. Bon appétit!